If you have ever visited a museum with displays of things then you've probably stopped to look at the mummies. Everyone is fascinated by these ancient bodies, all wrapped up in bandages and lying in their painted coffins. But have you ever wondered about what type of people they were when they were alive? What sort of work did they do? Were they married? Did they have any hobbies?

Meet the mummies

Because mummies are so old, it is easy to forget that they were once people just like us, with jobs and families, friends and pets, aches and pains, and even favourite foods, music and sports. In this book you will meet seven ancient Egyptians whose mummies are now in the British Museum, and some of the people who have helped us learn about their lives.

What is a mummy?

A mummy is a dead body that has been preserved by drying. Mummies don't have to be people – there are animal, bird, fish and even insect mummies, too! And they don't have to be Egyptian, either. Although all the people and animals in this book do come from Egypt, mummies are found in many places around the world.

How were mummies made?

The first Egyptians to be mummified were preserved by accident when they were buried in the desert. When others found them months or years later, their dead bodies had been dried out by the hot sand, leaving their skin, hair, teeth and nails looking just as they had in life. Perhaps this made the Egyptians wonder about life after death, because soon afterwards they decided that dead people needed their bodies for the afterlife. They learned to preserve bodies by drying them out with chemicals, covering them with resin and wrapping them in bandages. We call these preserved bodies 'mummies' because the Arabic word for the bitumen used in mummification is *mummiya*.

Our friends, the mummies

Some people are so used to seeing mummies in horror films or comics that they think of them as horrible monsters living in tombs. This is unfair. Not only has no mummy ever come back to life and hurt anyone, mummies can in fact be very helpful. Even though they can't talk to us, they can still tell us a lot – if we ask the right questions in the right way.

You could probably guess that mummies are good at telling us about life in ancient times – what people looked like, how long they lived, what they ate and what diseases they got. But did you know that mummies are also helping modern doctors to treat and prevent the illnesses and injuries people suffer from today? Or that a mummy probably helped you before you were born? As you'll discover, mummies really can be our friends!

Ginger

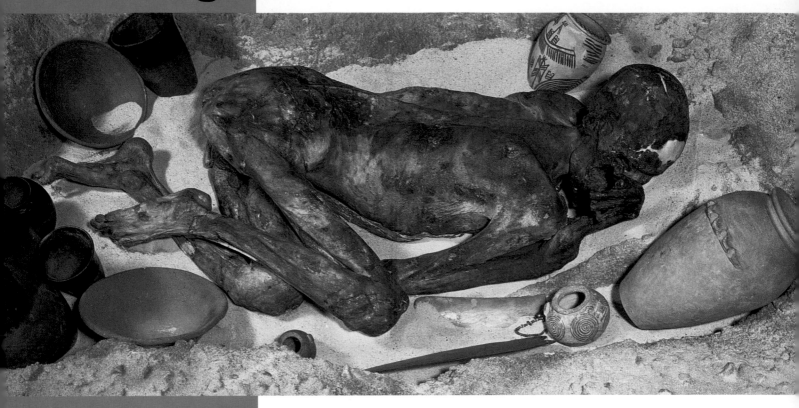

A Stone Age farmer, about 3400 BC

The oldest mummy in this book belongs to a man who died more than 5,000 years ago. There was no writing in prehistoric Egypt, so we don't know his name, but because of his red hair generations of people have called him 'Ginger'. We don't even know exactly how old he was when he died, but he probably wasn't much over thirty — very few people lived to an old age in his time. What we do know is that he must have believed in an afterlife, because his family filled his grave with all the things they thought he needed for the next world — food, tools and hunting weapons.

The first Egyptians

Like most of his people, Ginger was probably a farmer. The first Egyptians had been wandering hunters, but Ginger's people had discovered how to grow food in the rich black mud left behind after the Nile flooded each year. They settled along the river banks, building themselves villages of mud houses. Although they still fished and hunted for food, they also kept animals like goats and cows.

They grew fruit and vegetables to eat, wheat and barley for making bread and beer, and flax for weaving linen cloth. They were experts at making stone tools and weapons, and they also learned to make pots and baskets for storing food. Prehistoric Egyptians lived together in large family groups called clans. Sometimes there were fights between neighbouring villages, but at other times clans got along well and traded with each other.

A prehistoric mummy

Ginger was found in a prehistoric cemetery at Gebelein, in southern Egypt, in 1899. His naked body had been buried in a pit in the ground, surrounded by pots and flint tools. The sand that filled the pit had dried his body out, preserving it perfectly. The local people who found the grave sent for Sir Ernest Wallis Budge of the British Museum, who was staying nearby at the time. Budge paid for the body and had it sent to England. The next year, Ginger went on public show in the Museum.

The River Nile.

Model of an ancient Egyptian farmer.

5

Grave goods

Archaeologist Alexandra Whittaker examining and recording finds from a tomb.

We know how Ginger and his people lived only because of what archaeologists have discovered about prehistoric Egypt. Archaeologists are a bit like detectives, collecting evidence from ancient sites like villages and cemeteries. After carefully recording everything they find and where they find it, they use the information to piece together a picture of how things were long ago.

Loaves of bread from a tomb.

Clues from the grave

Things buried with the dead are called 'grave goods', and they are one of the most important ways of learning about ancient people and their lives.

Where archaeologists find grave goods, they know that the people buried there believed they would live after death, and what they thought they would need for the next life. Burial has preserved many things that would otherwise have been worn out or thrown away, such as clothes, food and furniture.

Tomb models

When the Egyptians couldn't put real things into tombs, they sometimes used clay or wooden models instead. They thought that a person would need a house in the next world, so they often placed a model house in the grave. Ginger's house, made of reeds and mud, would have been destroyed thousands of years ago, but because of models found in other tombs we know what it might have looked like.

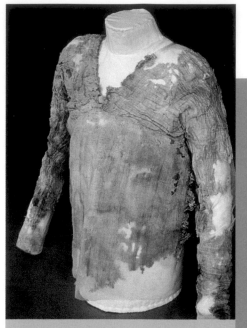

Linen dress from a tomb.

Pottery model of a house.

Stool from a tomb.

Timeline of ancient Egypt

Grave goods help archaeologists to work out the dates of people and places. Because they know that everything in a grave was put there at the same time, archaeologists can compare finds from different places to work out which came first and which came later. The time when Ginger lived is called 'predynastic', because it came before the 'dynasties', or families of kings, that later ruled Egypt.

5000 BC	**Predynastic Period** 5500 – 3100 BC
4000 BC	
3000 BC	
	Old Kingdom 2686 – 2181 BC
2000 BC	**Middle Kingdom** 2055 – 1650 BC
	New Kingdom 1550 – 1069 BC
1000 BC	
	Ptolemaic Period 332 – 32 BC
0	
	Roman Period 30 BC – AD 395
AD	

Mummies in the ancient world

Until the 19th century nobody knew how to read ancient Egyptian writing, even though other ancient languages were well understood. All educated people in the 18th and 19th centuries could read Greek and Latin, and sometimes Hebrew, too. Even people who did not know foreign languages could read English translations of the Bible and books by classical writers. Until Egyptologists learned to decipher ancient Egyptian scripts, most people got their ideas about what ancient Egypt was like from the Bible and from what the Greeks and Romans had written about it.

An Anglo-Saxon Bible manuscript showing the Israelites taking Joseph's mummy out of Egypt.

Most people in the ancient world used to bury their dead or cremate them. Of all the peoples living around the Mediterranean, only the Egyptians deliberately mummified their dead. This fascinated their neighbours, and many ancient authors wrote about

An Egyptian-style sarcophagus from Syria.

mummies and mummification. One of the earliest descriptions of mummification is found in the Bible. The Book of Genesis tells how Joseph and his father Jacob were mummified after they died in Egypt. Later on, when Moses led the Israelites out of Egypt, they took Joseph's mummy with them.

Eyewitness reports

Even today, a lot of what we know about mummification comes from the writings of ancient authors like Herodotus, a Greek traveller who visited Egypt in the 5th century BC. Herodotus was very interested in everything he saw, and he gave a long description of the different methods of mummification being practised in his time. About 400 years later another Greek, called Diodorus of Sicily, wrote about mummification in Roman times. Some Roman writers, including a Greek doctor called Dioscorides, believed that medicine made from mummified bodies was good for treating illnesses!

Egyptian style

After Egypt became a part of the Roman Empire in 30 BC, the Egyptian religion gained popularity throughout the Roman world. Romans worshipped Egyptian gods and goddesses like Osiris and Isis. Some Romans living in Egypt had themselves mummified and buried in Egyptian-style tombs. One Roman magistrate even built himself a tomb in the shape of a pyramid. Meanwhile, in Syria and Carthage, it became fashionable for rich people to be buried in Egyptian-style stone coffins.

A visit to the embalmers

Herodotus described what happened when someone died and the relatives took the body to the embalmers' workshop:

When a body is brought to them, the embalmers show the relatives wooden models of mummies, painted to look like the real thing … Having pointed out the differences between them, they ask in what way the body is to be prepared. After their relatives have agreed a price, they go away, leaving the embalmers to their work.

Herodotus, *The Histories,* Book Two, c. 450 BC.

The pyramid of Gaius Cestius in Rome.

Ankhef

A Middle Kingdom official, about 1950 BC

Ankhef lived and worked in Asyut, in the Nile Valley, during the time we call the Middle Kingdom. More than a thousand years had passed since Ginger's time, and many things had changed. Egypt was now one kingdom, stretching from the Mediterranean Sea in the north to the Nile Cataracts in the south. Because the country was so big, it had been divided into provinces ruled by governors. Asyut was the capital of Ankhef's province, so it is quite likely that he had a job working for the local governor, though we don't know exactly what he did.

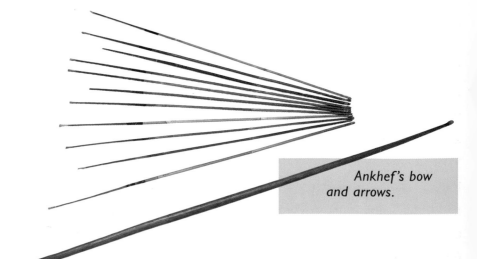

Ankhef's bow and arrows.

A statue of a Middle Kingdom official.

Ankhef's tomb was cut into the cliffs above the valley here in Asyut.

Like most Egyptians, Ankhef probably got married when he grew up. He was not very rich, but not poor, and he might even have been a landowner. We can guess that he liked hunting because he was buried with his bow and arrows lying on top of his coffin. We can also imagine what he looked like because his mummy mask shows him wearing a beard and moustache, which was the fashion at the time. We do know that Ankhef lived to be quite old because his teeth were worn down, and he had painful arthritis in his back and hip. The pain may have affected how he walked. It might even have made him rather grumpy!

By the time Ankhef died, the Egyptians had learned how to preserve bodies by drying them with a natural salt called natron and then wrapping them in linen bandages. Ankhef's mummy was found in 1907 by the English archaeologist David Hogarth. The tomb had been cut into the rock cliffs high above Asyut, and contained four coffins and a few offerings. Ankhef's coffin was tucked away in a tiny chamber at the back of the tomb, hidden by a wooden panel. Apart from his bow and arrows, Ankhef didn't have many grave goods, but his coffin was painted with prayers asking for offerings such as food, drink and clothes.

11

Tombs

Ancient Egyptian tombs can tell us as much about life in Egypt as the things we find inside them. When Ginger was buried, his grave was just covered with a pile of sand and stones, but later on, as the Egyptians' beliefs about the afterlife grew more sophisticated, these 'grave mounds' became larger and more elaborate. People started to think of tombs as homes where the dead went on living.

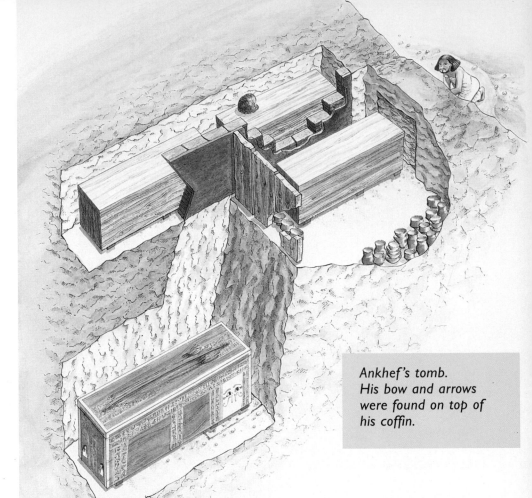

Ankhef's tomb. His bow and arrows were found on top of his coffin.

This Old Kingdom tomb at Giza looks a bit like the model house on page 7. Behind it is the pyramid tomb of King Khafra.

False doors were carved with pictures of offerings and prayers for the dead person. If something happened to the tomb owner's mummy, the statue could act as a substitute body.

A home for ever

Egyptians called their tombs 'Houses of Eternity' and made them look like the homes of the living. Although the houses where people lived were usually built of mud bricks, the Egyptians preferred to make their tombs from stone, because it lasted longer. Some tombs were built above ground; others, like Ankhef's, were cut into the cliffs of the Nile valley. Inside them there were rooms to store all the food, drink and clothes the dead people might need for the next life, and 'false doors' that allowed their spirits to go in and out of the burial chamber.

Royal tombs

Royal tombs were different from ordinary people's. Kings and queens were buried in pyramids or secret underground tombs. Magic spells and pictures were carved or painted on the walls to help them on their journey through the underworld. These scenes are very important in helping us understand the ancient Egyptian religion.

Tomb painting showing life in the Egyptian paradise.

Tomb paintings

In some tombs, the walls were carved or painted with scenes showing everything the tomb owners wanted to enjoy in the next world. As well as offerings such as food and drink, the paintings show people at work and play, worshipping the gods or drinking and gossiping at family parties. Tomb paintings tell us all kinds of things about Egyptian life, such as what people ate, how they dressed and how they did different sorts of work. Sometimes they even show what the Egyptians thought life would be like in the next world.

Painting from the underground tomb of King Horemheb in the Valley of the Kings. The king is worshipping the goddess Hathor, who welcomes him to the next world.

Explorers and archaeologists

When Hogarth excavated Ankhef's tomb, he was careful to keep a detailed record of everything he found and exactly where he found it. Modern archaeologists understand how important even the tiniest pieces of evidence can be, and they use all kinds of equipment – from cameras to computers – to record the smallest details of their discoveries. This is one reason why it sometimes takes many years to excavate a single tomb.

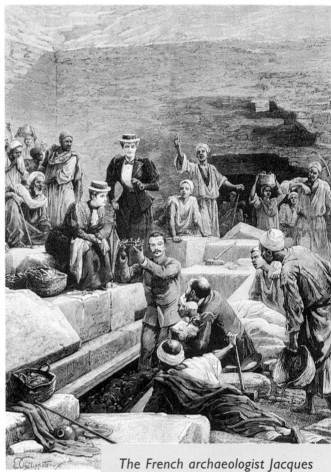

The French archaeologist Jacques de Morgan opening the coffin of an Egyptian princess in 1896.

Archaeologist Helen Strudwick copying paintings in a tomb at Thebes.

Tomb robbers

Things were not always this way. From ancient Egyptian times, robbers had broken into tombs looking for things to steal. They were only interested in the mummies' golden masks and jewellery. They ripped apart mummified bodies or set them on fire to get at the gold and precious stones hidden inside the bandages. For hundreds of years tombs were raided in search of treasure – in medieval times, there were even guide books published to help people be better tomb robbers!

The first Egyptologists

European travellers first started getting interested in Egypt during the Middle Ages, when Christian pilgrims visiting the Holy Land often stopped in Egypt to visit places mentioned in the Bible. The first important study of ancient Egypt was made by French scholars and engineers who went to Egypt with Napoleon in 1798. Among the discoveries they sent back to Paris were several mummies, and it was from about this time that mummies began to be studied seriously.

X-ray of the skull of an ancient Egyptian woman called Katebet (see page 16). It shows that she only had two teeth left when she died.

In the 19th century just about anybody could go to Egypt and, if they had enough money, start digging up tombs. Nobody really understood how important it was to record their discoveries, and it was not until the end of the century that the first proper Egyptologists had worked out systems for recording and handling their finds.

As more and more mummies found their way into museums around the world, scientific examinations became more common. At first this meant unwrapping the mummies, but once X-ray photography had been invented mummies could be investigated without damaging them.

Egyptologists are specialists in the study of ancient Egypt. This picture shows Egyptologists Joann Fletcher and David Depraeter excavating a prehistoric grave like Ginger's.

Katebet

A wealthy lady, about 1300 BC

Katebet was a wealthy lady who lived in Thebes in southern Egypt during the New Kingdom, when Egypt was rich and powerful. Thebes was one of the biggest and most important Egyptian cities. The main part, where most people lived and worked, was built on the east bank of the Nile. The cemeteries were on the west bank, because the Egyptians believed that the place where the sun set was the entrance to the underworld. Kings and princes were buried in the Valley of the Kings, their wives and other children in the Valley of the Queens. The tombs of people such as Katebet are called the Tombs of the Nobles. Katebet was buried with a man called Qenna, who may have been her husband. Their tomb did not have any paintings, but some of their grave goods were still there when it was discovered.

View across Thebes from the Tombs of the Nobles.

Tomb painting of ladies at a party in Thebes. They are wearing wigs like the one shown on Katebet's mask.

Hairpiece from Katebet's coffin.

We don't know any of the details of Katebet's life. The only thing we can say for sure is that she was more than fifty years old when she died, so she would have been considered a very old lady. But despite her age, she must still have cared about looking good, because she was buried with two hairpieces in her coffin! Like most ancient Egyptian women, Katebet probably married young and had a family.

Her main job would have been running her home, but there would have been lots of servants to do the hard work. When she died, Katebet had only two teeth left, so all her food must have been cut up small or mashed. This could have made her bad-tempered, but we can tell that her family still loved her because they took great care to prepare her for her burial.

17

Funeral equipment

Katebet's family went to great expense to make sure her mummy was well equipped for the afterlife. Her head, shoulders and chest were covered with a beautiful mask with real rings on the fingers. Charms called amulets were laid carefully on her body to protect her on her journey to the next world. A magic figure, called a shabti, was placed on her legs. Funeral equipment like this has helped Egyptologists to work out what the Egyptians believed about the afterlife and how they thought they should prepare for it.

Katebet's mummy mask.

Masks

Funeral masks were placed over the heads of the dead to protect them and help their spirits find their way back to their bodies. The face represented the way the dead person wanted to look in the next world, so Katebet's mask shows her looking young and beautiful, with golden skin, even though she was old when she died. The faces of mummy masks were often gilded or coloured gold. This is because the Egyptians believed that the flesh of the gods was made of gold.

Gold never rots or corrodes, but stays perfect for ever. The Egyptians hoped this magic quality would help to preserve their bodies and make them like gods, too.

Amulets

Amulets were magic charms worn for protection by the living as well as the dead. There were lots of different types of amulet, including small figures of gods and goddesses, magic symbols or small models of things people might need in the next life. For some amulets to work properly, a priest had to say magic spells over them in the proper way and at the proper time.

The knot amulet, or tyet, stood for the protection of the goddess Isis.

The djed pillar was the symbol of Osiris, the ruler of the underworld.

The jackal Anubis was the cemetery god and the protector of the dead.

Katebet's heart scarab.

Scarabs

One of the most popular amulets was a model of the scarab, or dung beetle, which lays its eggs inside balls of animal droppings. When the eggs hatch, the balls break apart and dozens of baby beetles run out. The Egyptians saw this and thought that the scarab could create new life by magic. It became their symbol of rebirth and they worshipped it as the rising sun that begins each new day. The scarab on Katebet's stomach is a special kind of amulet called a 'heart scarab' (see page 37).

Box of shabtis made for a high-ranking lady.

Shabtis

The little figure on Katebet's legs is called a shabti or ushabti, which means 'answerer'. Wealthy people like Katebet were not used to hard work, and they worried that after they died the god Osiris, who ruled the underworld, might ask them to work in his fields. So they equipped their tombs with magic figures who would do the work for them. Katebet's shabti carries a hoe for digging in the fields and a flail for threshing grain. Wealthy Egyptians were sometimes buried with whole boxes of shabtis. Some contained as many as 401 figures – 365 workers to provide labour each day of the year, and 36 overseers to supervise them!

Katebet's shabti.

Shabtis are usually inscribed with a magic spell that says:

O shabti allotted to me, if I am called or if I am detailed to do any work that has to be done in the realm of the dead ... you shall offer yourself for me on every occasion of cultivating the fields, flooding the banks or moving sand from east to west. 'Here I am!' you shall say.

Book of the Dead, Spell 6

The mummy trade

Katebet's mummy came to the British Museum in 1835. It was bought in a sale along with a lot of other Egyptian antiquities. Until recent times hardly anybody thought of mummies as people – they were just interesting objects to be bought and sold alongside other ancient curiosities. But in a way, Katebet has been lucky to survive at all. The body of Qenna, the man she was buried with, has disappeared without trace. The only way we know that he ever lived is from his name, written on a papyrus document from their tomb. It could be that Qenna was a victim of the gruesome mummy trade.

Mummy medicine

For hundreds of years, Egyptian tomb robbers made a living by stealing mummies from tombs and selling them to foreigners. The first Europeans to be interested in buying mummies were medieval apothecaries. Apothecaries were a bit like modern pharmacists, though they acted more like doctors, prescribing pills and potions for different illnesses.

This hand is all that survives of a mummy used for making medicine.

Real and fake mummy. The green box, used to hold powdered mummy, is labelled Mum[ia] Ver[a], Latin for 'true mummy'. The page is from a 17th-century book giving instructions for making 'philosophical' mummy, which was supposed to have the same effects as the real thing.

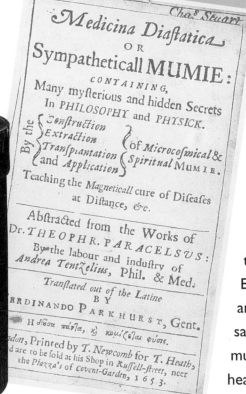

Apothecaries had no scientific training – their cures were a mixture of traditional remedies and magic. They had read about the ancient magicians of Egypt, and what Greek and Roman writers had said about ground-up mummies being used to heal diseases.

20

Marriage-A-la-Mode. (Plate III)

Invented Painted & Published by W. Hogarth —

Engraved by B. Baron

According to Act of Parliament, April 1st 1745.

Soon, powdered mummy became their favourite remedy for a huge range of complaints, including broken bones, concussion, paralysis, migraines, epilepsy, liver diseases, sore throats, coughs and boils.

Did it work?

There is no evidence that mummy medicine can cure anything at all, but perhaps people believed it was doing them good. Purging the body was thought to be very beneficial, and swallowing powdered mummy made patients violently sick. Once their vomiting had stopped, they probably did feel better!

Fake mummies

By the 18th century, the demand for mummy medicine had become so huge that there was a thriving business in fake mummies. Any dead body could be dried out and wrapped up to look like the real thing – until it began to rot and stink! To prevent faking, the Egyptian government put heavy taxes on the export of mummies, but they did not try to stop the trade altogether. Eventually, new medical discoveries in the 19th century led to mummy medicine going out of fashion, though this did not stop people collecting mummies for other reasons.

An eyewitness account of the mummy trade:

Without the Citie, six miles higher into the land, are to be seene neere unto the river diverse Piramides, among which are three marvellous great, and very artificially wrought. Out of one of these are dayly digged the bodies of auncient men, not rotten but all whole, the cause whereof is the qualitie of the Egyptian soile, which will not consume the flesh of man, but rather dry and harden the same, and so always conserveth it. And these dead bodies are the Mummie which the Phisitians and Apothecaries doe against our willes make us swallow.

Anonymous visitor to Cairo, about 1580.
From Hakluyt's *Principal Voyages*, London 1598–1600

A Theban noblewoman

about 700 BC

Although this lady's name is a mystery, we do know that she probably lived in Thebes in about 700 BC. Like Katebet, she was quite old when she died, but we have no idea where she was buried or whether she had any grave goods. However, we can also tell from her beautifully-mummified body that she must have been very rich, because only the wealthiest people could afford the best embalming. So, although we don't know the details of her life, we can imagine what it was like by looking at how other wealthy women in Thebes lived at this time.

Luxor temple was the temple of Amun in southern Thebes.

A royal priestess of Amun.

Women at work

As well as running their homes, many women had jobs outside the house. There is no proof that girls were taught to read and write, but this did not stop women from working, owning houses, farms and animals, or running businesses such as linen workshops and market gardens.

Wealthy women worked, too; some ran their own estates or businesses, while others were part-time priestesses in the temples of Egypt's many gods and goddesses.

Thebes was the home of Egypt's chief god, Amun, and many Theban noblewomen served as priestesses in his temples. When this lady was alive, the chief priestesses of Amun were usually royal princesses and they ruled the south of Egypt like queens.

An ancient celebrity

In 1873, a few years after she was brought to England, our noblewoman was unwrapped in London by the famous anatomist Sir Richard Owen. Her mummy proved to be a superb example of the Egyptian embalmers' skill and provided lots of information about how mummification was done. After the unwrapping, our noblewoman was presented to the British Museum. She arrived in a coffin made for a man who was a priest of Montu, the Theban war god, but the reason for this, like her name, remains a mystery . . .

23

In this tomb painting an embalming priest dressed as the god Anubis puts the finishing touches to a mummy.

Plaques like this were placed over the incision through which the embalmers removed the internal organs. They were marked with the eye of the god Horus to stop evil spirits entering the body.

Mummies

A bag of natron.

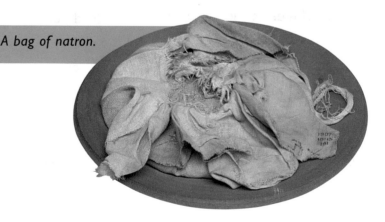

In Egypt's hot climate, it was important to get a dead person to the embalmers' workshop as quickly as possible, before the body began to decay. Different qualities of treatment were available, depending on what the person's family could afford. The cheapest methods involved dissolving the body's insides, then drying it out. The best and most expensive treatment – the kind that our noblewoman received – was a lot more complicated.

Mummification

Egyptian embalmers had discovered that it was the internal organs rotting that made a body decay, so after washing a corpse the first thing they did was to remove the insides through a cut made in the left side.

The dead person's insides were embalmed and bandaged separately. The heart was left in the body so that it could be judged by Osiris in the next world. Sometimes the lungs, liver, intestines and stomach were put in special vases called canopic jars, but our noblewoman's organs were put back inside her. Other parts of the body were not kept – sometimes the brain was scraped out through the nose or a hole in the skull and buried with other left-over bits.

Once the insides had been removed, the embalmers washed the body again and then covered it with a special type of salt called natron. After forty days, the natron had soaked up all the moisture in the tissues and dissolved all the fat and muscles, leaving the body dark and shrivelled. The embalmers washed the body out once more, then stuffed it with linen or sawdust to make it look more lifelike. Sweet-smelling herbs and spices were added to the filling to take away any bad smells.

Finishing touches

The embalmers massaged the mummy's skin with perfumed oils, and covered the cut in the side with a special plaque. Then they coated the whole body with melted resin to make it strong and waterproof. They made the dead person look as nice as possible by doing the hair and putting make-up on the face. The finished mummy was wrapped up in linen sheets and bandages.

Special jewellery was placed on the body, and amulets were tucked between the wrappings to protect the dead person on the journey to the next life. Last of all, the embalmers covered the dead person's face with a funeral mask and carefully laid the mummy in its coffin, ready for the relatives to collect on the day of the funeral.

A wrapped mummy.

Canopic jars. The lids represent four gods called the Sons of Horus, who protected the dead person's organs.

Mummy madness

The discoveries of explorers and archaeologists in Egypt during the 18th and 19th centuries created great interest and excitement among the public in America and Europe. Wealthy invalids were encouraged to spend the winters in Egypt's warm, dry climate, and it soon became fashionable for rich people to go there on holiday. Some were genuinely interested in ancient Egypt and became respected Egyptologists or patrons themselves. Many more, however, just wanted to collect stories and souvenirs to impress their friends at home.

This painting by the 19th-century artist Degas shows a young woman in her father's study. Behind her is a glass case full of Egyptian objects.

A present from Egypt

It might seem strange now, but the most popular souvenirs were human and animal mummies. Not wanting to disappoint important visitors, the Egyptian authorities and tour organizers began arranging for collections of mummies to be buried in places where they could be 'discovered'! Back in Europe and America, wealthy people displayed mummies in their houses as proof of how well-travelled and learned they were. Meanwhile the public flocked to see mummy exhibitions staged by explorers and antiquity-hunters. Some collectors went even further, arranging parties at which mummies were unwrapped in front of their guests.

The pioneer Egyptologist Margaret Murray unwrapping a mummy in 1908.

The Nobility and Gentry, Visiters and Inhabitants of BATH and its Vicinity, are respectfully informed, that

TWO EGYPTIAN
MUMMIES,
A MALE AND FEMALE,
In the highest State of Preservation, with various other Relics,
BROUGHT TO THIS COUNTRY BY
Mr. BELZONI,
The celebrated Traveller, are now open for Exhibition at
10, New Bond-Street.

The MUMMIES are of the first Class: the Inspection of them it is presumed must highly satisfactory to every Person, as exhibiting two distinct Specimens; the ndages of the Male having been entirely removed from the Body, which is perfect, le the mode of applying them is beautifully illustrated in the Envelope of the Female. The CASES are covered with Hieroglyphics, enriched with Ornaments most rately executed; the Interiors containing the Histories of the Lives of their very nt Occupiers, in Egyptian Characters, as fresh as when inscribed by the Hand of rtist, after a Lapse of probably

THREE THOUSAND YEARS.

"Perchance that very Hand, now pinioned flat,
"Has hob-a-nob'd with Pharaoh glass to glass,
"Or dropp'd a halfpenny in Homer's hat,
"Or doff'd its own to let Queen Dido pass,
"Or held, by Solomon's own invitation,
"A torch at the great Temple's dedication."

AMONG THE OTHER RELICS WILL BE FOUND

A MUMMY OF THE IBIS,
THE SACRED BIRD OF EGYPT;
Urn with Intestines from Elei ; an Inscription on the far-famed Paper of Egypt (the massive Fragment of Granite with Hieroglyphics from Memphis ; a variety of Idols in and Wood, from the Tombs of the Kings in the Valley of Beban-el-Malook, and the nc ; Urns, Vessels of Libation, Bronzes, Coins, &c. &c.

A few EGYPTIAN and other ANTIQUITIES for SALE.
Admittance, One Shilling each.
☞ PURCHASERS WILL BE ALWAYS RE-ADMISSIBLE.
RIPTIVE ACCOUNT of this COLLECTION will
WOOD and CO. Printers of the Bath and Chelt...

LORD LONDESBOROUGH
At Home,
MONDAY, 10th JUNE, 1850,
144, PICCADILLY.
A Mummy from Thebes to be unrolled at half-past Two.
To
No.

Invitation to a mummy unwrapping.

Exhibitions of mummies were a popular attraction in the 19th century.

Mummies on show

These parties became so popular that a craze began for public unwrappings, where mummies were dissected in front of huge paying audiences. The most famous promoter of public unwrappings was Thomas 'Mummy' Pettigrew, who performed many unwrappings in England in the 1830s and 1840s. He soon found some mummies were more difficult to unwrap than others – once he had to saw one apart to get inside it!

Funeral fashions

Even weirder was the 19th-century fashion for rich people to have themselves mummified. In 1852, 'Mummy' Pettigrew mummified the body of the Duke of Hamilton, who had requested it in his will.

Even people who weren't mummified were affected by the mummy craze – some were buried in Egyptian coffins, and many chose Egyptian designs for their tombs. This is why 19th-century cemeteries are often full of monuments shaped like pyramids, obelisks and Egyptian temples.

This Egyptian obelisk marks the tomb of Jean-François Champollion, who deciphered hieroglyphs.

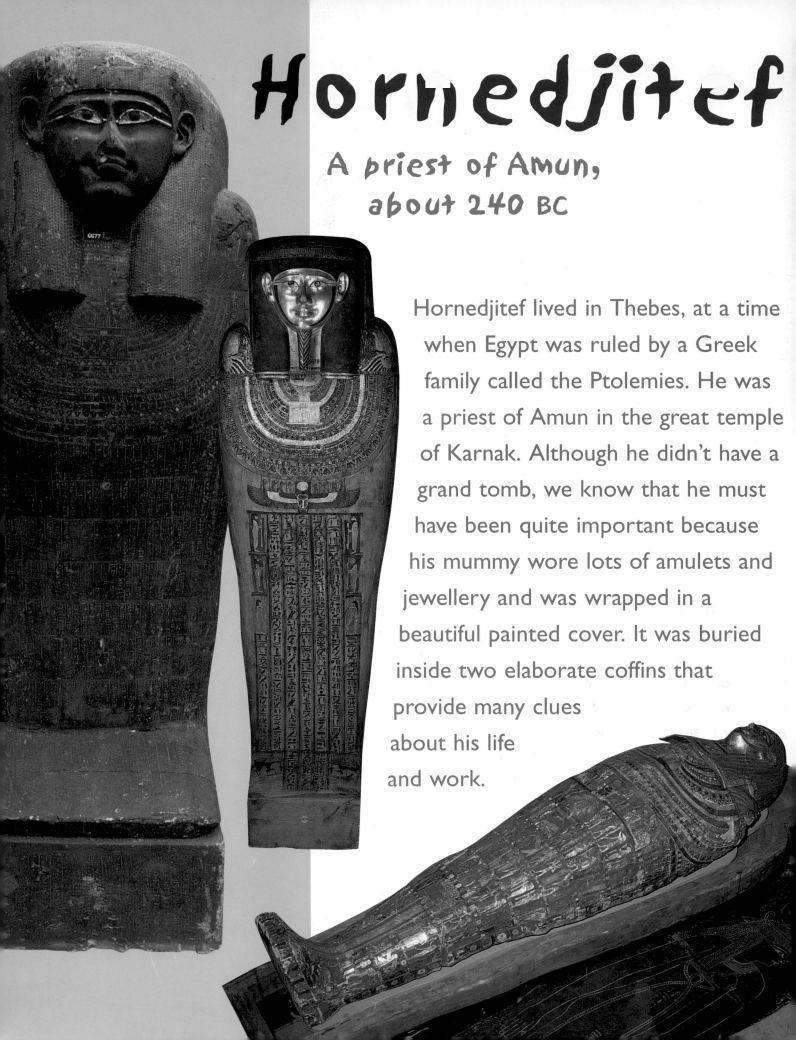

Hornedjitef

A priest of Amun, about 240 BC

Hornedjitef lived in Thebes, at a time when Egypt was ruled by a Greek family called the Ptolemies. He was a priest of Amun in the great temple of Karnak. Although he didn't have a grand tomb, we know that he must have been quite important because his mummy wore lots of amulets and jewellery and was wrapped in a beautiful painted cover. It was buried inside two elaborate coffins that provide many clues about his life and work.

The temple of Amun at Karnak.

Bronze figure of a priest.

Egyptian religion

The Egyptians had many gods and goddesses who they believed would look after them – as long as they were content. If a god or goddess was angry with someone, he or she might make that person ill or even kill them. If the gods were angry with the whole country, they might start a war or stop the Nile from rising high enough to water the fields. To keep the gods and goddesses happy, the Egyptians built them beautiful temples where their statues were worshipped.

Temples

The Egyptians believed that the statues in temples were really the bodies of the gods and goddesses, and the priests and priestesses were like their servants. Every day, they bathed and dressed the divine images, put make-up and perfume on them, offered them incense and served them delicious meals. All this activity meant that temples were like small, busy towns, with stores, offices, workshops, libraries, kitchens and schools for training scribes and priests. The local government

offices and law courts were often part of the temple, too, and the priests were in charge of collecting taxes for the government. In return, they were paid with shares of the offerings given to the gods and goddesses.

Priests on duty in the temple had to follow lots of rules. They had to live apart from their wives, shave all the hair from their heads and bodies and take two cold baths every day!

Coffins and sarcophagi

Homes for the dead

Coffins were usually made of wood, but rich people sometimes had an outer coffin made of stone. This is called a sarcophagus, a Greek word meaning 'flesh-eating'. (The Greeks thought that stone sarcophagi made bodies decompose.) Like tombs, coffins and sarcophagi were thought of as homes for the dead. Early coffins and sarcophagi looked a bit like houses, with false doors for the dead person's spirit to come and go. People's names were written on the outside to help their spirits find their way back if they went outside.

Providing for the afterlife

The writing and paintings on coffins tell us about the things people wanted to have in the next life – some of the things Ankhef asked for on his coffin were bread, beer and linen clothes. Coffins were also meant to protect the dead on their journey through the next world, and some have magic spells and pictures of gods and goddesses painted on them.

Katebet's coffin.

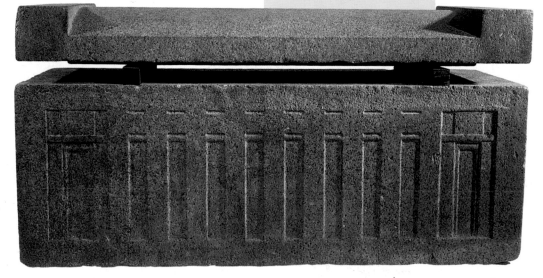

This sarcophagus was made to look like a house, with false doors at either end.

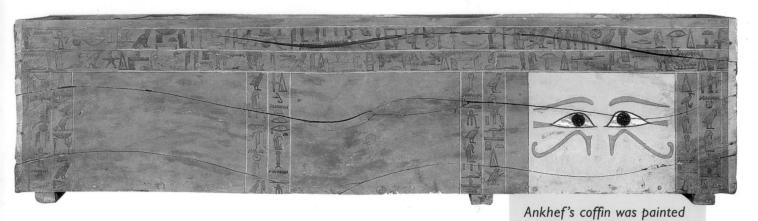

Ankhef's coffin was painted with prayers asking for offerings, and eyes to let his spirit see out.

Later on, coffins were made to look like the dead person. That way, if anything happened to the mummy, the coffin could act as a substitute body. People were shown wearing heavy wigs and big collars, with their arms crossed over their chest. Sometimes their faces were painted green or black, like the face of Osiris, the god of the dead. The whole of Hornedjitef's massive outer coffin was painted black, with gold writing, but his inner coffin was painted in bright colours with pictures of gods and goddesses. You can see both coffins on page 28.

In Roman times, mummy cases were sometimes quite realistic, showing the dead person almost as they were in life. Mummy cases like these can tell us lots about fashion, jewellery and hairstyles in Roman Egypt.

Mummy case of a young Roman girl.

A Promise for Eternity

One of the magic spells on Hornedjitef's coffin came with this guarantee for safe passage and food in the afterlife:

As for him who knows this book on earth or it is put in writing on the coffin, it is my word that he shall go out into the day in any shape that he desires and shall go into his place without being turned back, and there shall be given to him bread and beer and a portion of meat from upon the altar of Osiris.

Book of the Dead, Spell 72

31

The mummy's curse

Hornedjitef's mummy was discovered at Thebes in the 1820s by diggers working for Henry Salt, the British Consul in Egypt. After Salt died, his collection was sold, and in 1835 Hornedjitef and his coffins were bought by the British Museum. It was also about this time that horror stories about mummies started to become popular. The Victorians loved creepy tales, and soon famous horror writers, such as Edgar Allan Poe, began writing spooky stories about mummies coming to life.

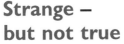

The 'Unlucky Mummy'.

A tomb curse

Some ancient Egyptian tombs really did have curses written on them, probably as warnings to frighten tomb robbers away. One of them reads:

As for any people who would enter this tomb unclean and do something evil to it, there will be judgment against them by the Great God!

Unwelcome guests

After reading these stories, many of the people who had been so keen to bring mummies back from their holidays in Egypt began to wonder whether they wanted them in their houses any more. What if they were haunted or brought bad luck? Some collectors decided the best thing to do was to give their mummies and coffins to museums, but once stories about them had started, there was no stopping them – and the myth of the mummy's curse was born.

Strange – but not true

Visitors to the British Museum still ask about the 'Unlucky Mummy', which is actually a coffin lid given to the Museum in 1889. According to the story that went around at the time, the 'mummy' had caused death and disaster wherever it went. All four of the people who brought it from Egypt had been killed or injured, and even the man who delivered it to the Museum was said to have died within the week. When it was photographed, the picture came out with an evil-looking face, and the photographer went mad and killed himself. Frightened museum staff said that the mummy made weird noises in the night and asked for it to be taken away, so it was sold to an American. It was loaded aboard the Titanic and, of course, the ship hit an iceberg and sank. The amazing thing is that none of this is true – the coffin lid has never hurt anybody and it is still in the Museum where you can visit it – if you dare . . .

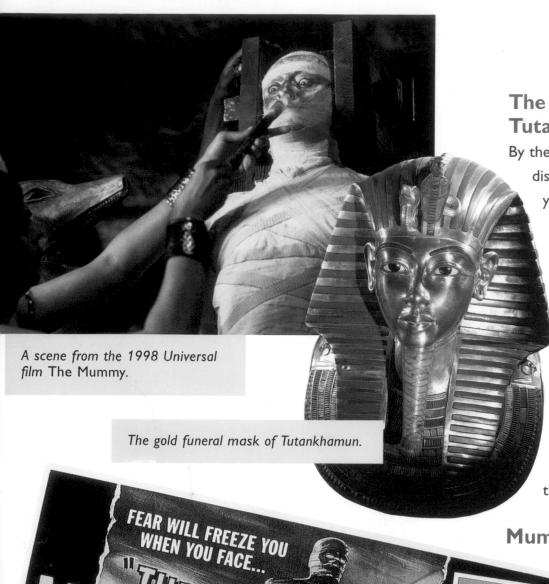

A scene from the 1998 Universal film The Mummy.

The gold funeral mask of Tutankhamun.

A poster for Hammer Films' 1959 mummy movie.

The curse of Tutankhamun

By the time that Howard Carter discovered the tomb of the young king Tutankhamun in the 1920s, many people firmly believed in the mummy's curse. When Carter's sponsor, Lord Carnarvon, died suddenly, people thought that a curse must have been responsible. Although Carter himself lived to be 65, this fact didn't stop the story about the curse spreading!

Mummy movies

Tales like this have made mummies essential characters in horror films for many years. The first mummy film was made in 1909, but the best known one, *The Mummy*, was made in 1932. It starred the famous horror actor Boris Karloff as Imhotep, a priest who was mummified alive for falling in love with a princess. The story was so popular that a new version was made in 1998, with extra-scary special effects.

A sacred ibis

about
150 BC

A sacred ibis.

Many of the mummies in museums today are not people, but birds and animals. Because the Egyptians lived so close to nature, they often depicted their gods and goddesses in the forms of the creatures they saw around them. The sacred ibis was identified with Thoth, the god of learning, and Thoth was often shown as an ibis-headed human.

Sacred animals

Our ibis comes from the sacred animal cemetery at Saqqara, close to the ancient Egyptian capital Memphis. The most important building at Saqqara is the Step Pyramid, built for King Djoser around 2650 BC. It was such an amazing monument that its architect Imhotep became a god identified with Thoth. As well as being the god of learning, Thoth was a god of medicine, and the Greeks identified him with their god of healing Asklepios. In Greek and Roman times, sick people often made pilgrimages to sacred sites like Saqqara to ask this god for a cure. One of the ways they tried to please him was to offer him a mummified ibis. At Saqqara, more than 10,000 ibises were buried in underground catacombs every year.

The underground tombs of the sacred ibises at Saqqara contain millions of mummified birds stacked on top of each other.

Temple carving of the god Thoth.

Coffin for a mummified ibis.

Mummy fraud

To supply these huge numbers of birds, sacred ibises were bred on a nearby lake and reared in special enclosures. While they were alive, the birds were well fed and cared for, but whenever new mummies were required, they would be killed and embalmed. Providing mummified ibises for pilgrims was big business for the priests, and sometimes they were tempted to cheat. Pilgrims bought the ibis mummies ready-packed inside pots or coffins, so they had no way of knowing what was inside.

Sometimes what they got was an empty jar!

Writing

How can we possibly know that over 2,000 years ago some crooked priests were faking ibis mummies at Saqqara? The answer is that somebody told on them. A priest called Hor was so shocked at his colleagues' behaviour that he reported their crimes to the authorities. As a result, six priests were arrested and put in prison. We know all this because the documents relating to the case were written on bits of pottery called ostraca.

The Rosetta Stone was made at about the time our ibis was alive.

An ostracon from the archive of the priest Hor.

Written documents are one of the most important sources of information about ancient Egypt because they tell us exactly what the ancient Egyptians thought, said and did. But until the 19th century nobody could make any sense of ancient Egyptian writing. Then the discovery of the Rosetta Stone changed everything. Inscribed on this slab of stone was the same text in ancient Greek and Egyptian. Because scholars could read the Greek, it provided the key to deciphering the mysterious Egyptian scripts.

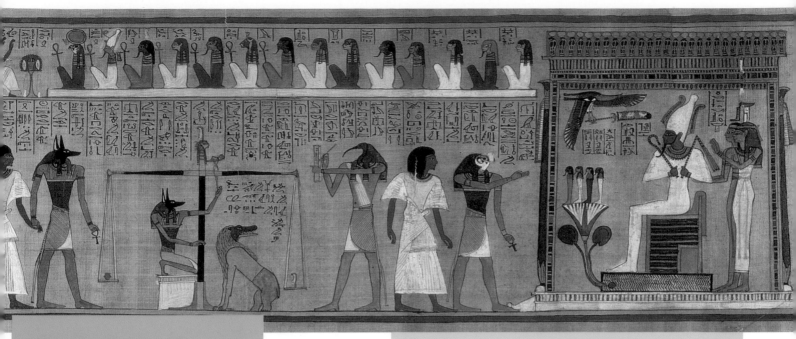

A papyrus Book of the Dead showing the scribe Hunefer's heart being weighed in front of Osiris. Ibis-headed Thoth records the verdict.

Heart scarabs

The Egyptians thought that a person's heart held a record of everything they had done in life, and that when the person died, the gods would test it to find out how he or she had behaved. Egyptians believed that dead people were taken to the court of Osiris, where their hearts were weighed against the Feather of Truth. If someone's heart was lighter than the feather, it meant that person had been good and would live forever in the Fields of Reeds, the Egyptian paradise. But if the heart was weighed down by bad deeds, it was eaten by a terrible monster and that person ceased to exist. To stop their hearts from revealing their bad deeds, the dead were equipped with special heart scarabs inscribed with a magic spell. Part of it reads:

O my heart which I had from my mother! Do not stand up as a witness against me ... Do not oppose me in the court!

Book of the Dead, Spell 30B

Books of the Dead

Not long after Ginger's time, more than 5,000 years ago, the Egyptians had begun to write their language down using signs called 'hieroglyphs', which means

The back of Katebet's heart scarab, showing the spell to protect her in the judgement hall of Osiris.

'sacred carvings'. Hieroglyphs on tombs, coffins and sarcophagi are very useful to Egyptologists because they usually give the name and the job of the dead person. We only know Ankhef and Katebet's names because they were written on their coffins.

Magic spells written in tombs and on funeral equipment, like amulets, were there to protect and provide for the dead person on the journey into the next world. Collections of these spells are known as Books of the Dead. Books of the Dead written on papyrus paper were put with mummies inside their coffins to act as guidebooks to the afterlife.

Mummies and museums

Although mummy medicine went out of fashion by the 19th century, there was still a flourishing trade in mummies. The craze for mummy souvenirs was in full swing – in 1833 a French priest told Mohammed Ali, the ruler of Egypt, that 'it would hardly be respectable, on one's return from Egypt, to present oneself without a mummy in one hand and a crocodile in the other'!

Children visiting Ginger in the British Museum.

This mummified cat was part of a cargo shipped to England for fertilizer.

The mummy business

In Egypt mummies were so common that for centuries they had been burnt as fuel for cooking and heating. In the 19th century enterprising businessmen found more profitable uses for them. Mummies were stripped of their bandages to supply rags for paper mills, and their bodies were ground up to make fertilizer. Millions of animal mummies – mostly cats and ibises – were sent to Europe as ballast weighing down the holds of ships. When they arrived, they too were sold as fertilizer. Powdered mummy was even used to make a kind of paint called 'Mummy Brown'. When one artist found out that the paint he was using had been made from dead bodies, he was so upset that he took it outside and gave it a proper burial in the garden!

Understanding mummies

In 1822 the French scholar Jean-François Champollion discovered the key to deciphering hieroglyphs, enabling Egyptologists around the world to study ancient Egyptian culture properly for the first time. They started to understand that mummies were an important source of evidence about life and death in ancient Egypt and realized how important it was to take care of them. As ordinary people learned more about ancient Egypt, they flocked to displays of mummies in museums, eager to see these survivors from ancient times.

Conservation and display

Today, mummies are more popular than ever. In many countries, ancient Egypt is studied as part of the school curriculum and the Egyptian galleries of museums are always crowded with people visiting the mummies. To preserve them for the future, mummies in museums are displayed in carefully-controlled environments and cared for by conservators who keep them in the best possible condition. As long as we look after our mummies, they will be able to share more and more of their secrets with our scientists and researchers.

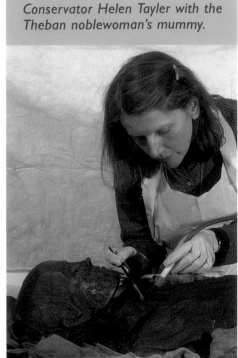

Conservator Helen Tayler with the Theban noblewoman's mummy.

The mummy gallery at the British Museum in 1847.

A Roman schoolboy

about AD 120

Although many of the people in this book lived to be quite old, this was fairly unusual. Many Egyptians did not survive childhood and those who did usually died in their thirties. This mummy belongs to a boy who lived during the 2nd century AD in a town called Philadelphia. Some Egyptians had become Christians by this time, but most still believed in their ancient religion, and people were still mummified to preserve their bodies for the next life. It was not until Christianity became Egypt's official religion in the fourth century AD that mummification finally died out.

Roman mummies

By Roman times, mummification was done less carefully, but more attention was given to how mummies looked on the outside. Instead of burying dead relatives, wealthy families kept their mummies above ground, in shrines or chapels where they could visit them. The mummies were elegantly wrapped with intricate patterns of bandages, and instead of mummy masks, their faces were covered with portraits painted on wood, clay or plaster.

The remains of classrooms in a Roman school at Alexandria.

Our schoolboy's portrait shows him as an adolescent, dressed in the Roman style.

We don't know why this boy died so young, because his body was already decomposing by the time he was mummified. One explanation is that he might have had an accident, but some Egyptologists think that the deep shadows under his eyes in his portrait suggest a fatal illness.

Children in Roman Egypt played with simple toys like this wooden cat.

Life in Roman Egypt

Philadelphia is in a region called the Fayum, one of the most prosperous parts of Egypt. Many farms in the Fayum were owned by retired Greek and Roman soldiers who had married Egyptian women. These families enjoyed a higher status than ordinary Egyptians. They were richer and did not have to pay so much tax. Our boy probably belonged to one of these privileged families. As a small child he would have stayed at home, playing with his toys, but from about the age of ten, he would have gone to a local school to study mathematics, Greek and Latin grammar and the works of classical Greek and Roman authors such as Homer and Virgil. Like any Roman schoolboy, he would also have trained in sports such as running, jumping, boxing and wrestling.

Mummy portraits

Our schoolboy's mummy was found by the British archaeologist William Flinders Petrie at Hawara, Philadelphia's cemetery, in 1888. Roman mummies were usually kept in family shrines, but when these became too crowded, the extra mummies were taken out and buried in pits in the ground. Petrie's team uncovered dozens of these pits, including the one containing the boy's mummy. Petrie found so many mummies at Hawara that he usually threw the bodies away, keeping just the heads and the portraits. Collecting mummies was no longer so fashionable, but the portraits were light and easy to transport – and Petrie knew that art collectors in Europe and America would be willing to pay high prices for them. The money he raised this way made it possible for him to carry on working in Egypt for many more years.

The schoolboy's realistic portrait clearly shows his Roman hairstyle and the creamy-white mantle he is wearing.

Petrie described his discovery at Hawara like this:

So soon as I went there I observed a cemetery on the north of the pyramid; on digging in it I saw that it was all Roman, the remains of brick tomb-chambers; and I was going to give it up as not worth working, when one day a mummy was found, with a painted portrait on a wooden panel placed over its face . . . More men were put onto this region, and in two days another portrait-mummy was found; in two days more a third, and then for nine days not one; an anxious waiting, suddenly rewarded by finding three. Generally three or four were found every week, and I have even rejoiced over five in one day. Altogether sixty were found in clearing this cemetery, some much decayed and worthless, others as fresh as the day they were painted.

(W.M. Flinders Petrie, *Ten Years Digging in Egypt*, 1893)

Painted plaster portrait mask of a Roman man.

Faces from the past

Mummy portraits were the first paintings to show the faces of ancient Egyptian people in a realistic way, along with accurate details of their clothes, hairstyles and jewellery.

With techniques borrowed from modern forensic scientists, archaeologists can use mummy portraits to reconstruct the faces of real people living in Egypt 2,000 years ago. First, a cast is made of the dead person's skull. Metal rods are added to mark the usual thickness of fat and muscle around the face and head, and then a sculptor begins to build up the person's features out of modelling clay, using the portrait as a guide. Finally, hair is added and the model is coloured to make it look as lifelike as possible.

This model head of a Roman lady was reconstructed from her mummy portrait.

Facial reconstruction: the head of an Egyptian man called Horemkenesi, based on a cast of the original skull. The plaster and clay 'half-head' (right) shows how the model was built up.

43

Mummies in medicine

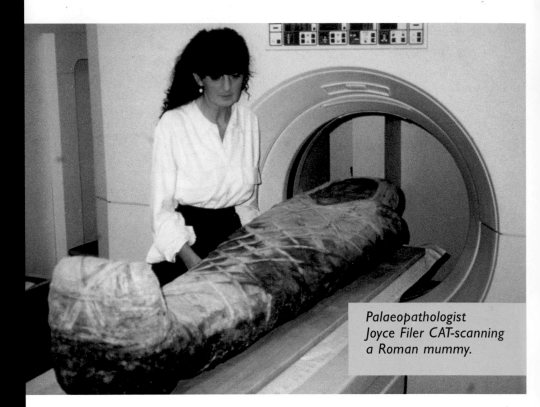

Palaeopathologist Joyce Filer CAT-scanning a Roman mummy.

CAT scan of the mummy of a man called Djedhor.

Until the 19th century, the only way mummies had contributed to medicine was by being ground up and swallowed! Today, they contribute in a very different way, by providing doctors with evidence of accidents and illnesses in ancient times and by helping them to develop new ways of diagnosing and treating sick people.

Mummy volunteers

CAT scanning (Computerized Axial Tomography) is now a vital tool for diagnosing diseases in living people, but mummies played a crucial role in developing the technology that has made this possible. CAT scanning works by taking a series of X-rays of thin sections across the patient's body, all the way from the head to the toes. A computer program then combines all these pictures to produce 3-D images of the person's insides.

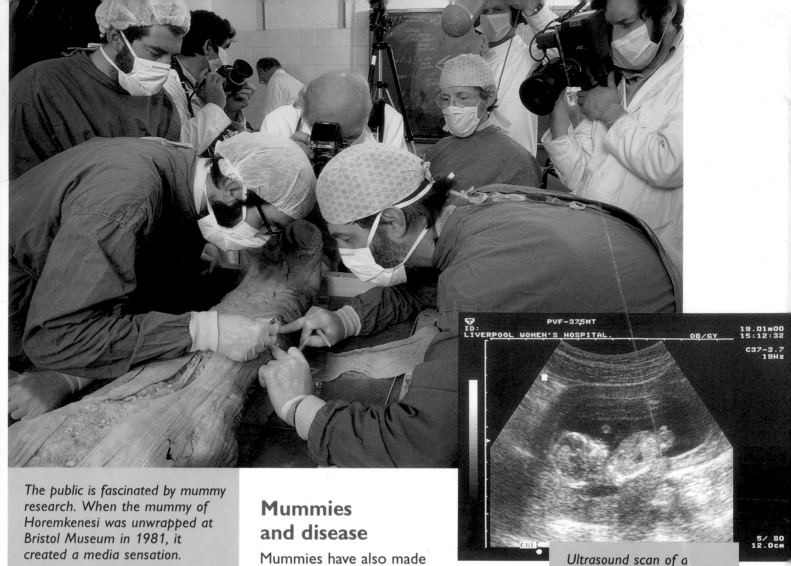

The public is fascinated by mummy research. When the mummy of Horemkenesi was unwrapped at Bristol Museum in 1981, it created a media sensation.

Ultrasound scan of a 12-week-old unborn baby.

Mummies and disease

Mummies have also made it possible for modern doctors to study diseases from ancient times. Using a technique called endoscopy, they insert a tube with a miniature camera attached into the mummy to snip off tissue from inside it. Doctors analyse this tissue to learn more about the diseases suffered by the ancient Egyptians. Many of these diseases, such as hepatitis, malaria and bilharzia, still kill people in Egypt and other countries. Doctors hope that by studying how these diseases evolved in ancient times they will discover clues to help them develop life-saving cures.

Because a mummy can be given high doses of radiation that would kill a living person, doctors developing scanning techniques used mummies to work out the best way to get clear images of internal organs and bones. At the same time, they discovered that CAT-scanning mummies gave them a clearer picture of complicated injuries like skull fractures. This has helped doctors to develop new surgical procedures.

Mummies and babies

You probably didn't know about it, but the chances are that a mummy helped you before you were even born! Most pregnant mothers today are given an ultrasound scan to check that their unborn babies are healthy. The computer programs that make it possible to see and photograph a baby inside its mother's womb were developed from the ones used to electronically 'unwrap' CAT-scanned mummies.

Further reading

For younger readers:

Harriet Griffey, *Secrets of the Mummies*, Dorling Kindersley Eyewitness Readers, London, 1998

Geraldine Harris and Delia Pemberton, *British Museum Illustrated Encyclopaedia of Ancient Egypt*, British Museum Press, London, 1999

James Putnam, *Mummy*, Dorling Kindersley Eyewitness Guides, London, 1993

For older readers:

Carol Andrews, *Egyptian Mummies*, British Museum Press, London, 1998

F. Dunard and R. Lichtenberg, *Mummies: A Journey Through Eternity*, Thames and Hudson New Horizons, London, 1998

Joyce Filer, *Disease*, British Museum Press Egyptian Bookshelf series, London, 1995

Salima Ikram and Aidan Dodson, *The Mummy in Ancient Egypt*, Thames and Hudson, London, 1998

Christine el Mahdy, *Mummies, Myths and Magic*, Thames and Hudson, London, 1995

John Taylor, *Unwrapping a Mummy*, British Museum Press Egyptian Bookshelf series, London, 1995

Susan Walker and Morris Bierbrier, *Ancient Faces: Mummy Portraits from Roman Egypt*, British Museum Press, London, 1997

Glossary

Abydos An important Egyptian city where Osiris was worshipped.

Alexandria The capital of Egypt in Greek and Roman times.

Amulet A protective charm.

Anubis The jackal-headed god of embalming and cemeteries.

Apothecary An old-fashioned pharmacist.

Book of the Dead A collection of magic spells to protect the dead in the next world.

Canopic jars Special jars for holding a mummy's internal organs.

Catacombs Underground rooms used for burials.

Conservator Someone who looks after ancient objects to keep them in the best possible condition.

Dynasty A ruling family. Thirty dynasties of kings and queens ruled over Egypt between 3100 BC and 343 BC.

Egyptologist Someone who studies ancient Egypt – that includes you now!

False Door A dummy door in a tomb or on a coffin or sarcophagus.

Fields of Reeds The Egyptian paradise.

Giza One of the cemeteries of Memphis.

Hieroglyphs Egyptian picture-writing.

Horus The falcon-headed god of kingship, son of Osiris and Isis.

Isis The goddess of magic, wife of Osiris and mother of Horus.

Memphis The ancient capital of Egypt.

Natron A salt used in mummification, a natural combination of sodium carbonate (washing soda) and sodium bicarbonate (baking soda).

Osiris The god of the dead. He is shown like a mummy with a black or green face.

Palaeopathologist Someone who studies ancient disease.

Papyrus A kind of paper made from stems of the papyrus reed.

Saqqara One of the cemeteries of Memphis.

Sarcophagus A stone coffin.

Scarab A beetle-shaped amulet.

Shabti A model worker to help the dead in the next life.

Sons of Horus Four gods who protected a mummy's internal organs. Hapy, with an ape's head, looked after the lungs. Imsety, with a man's head, looked after the liver. Qebehsenuef, with a hawk's head, looked after the intestines. Duamutef, with a jackal's head, looked after the stomach.

Thebes An important city in southern Egypt, now called Luxor.

Thoth The ibis-headed god of learning, writing and medicine.